Snap books

Top FOOTBALL Tips

DANIELLE HAMMELEF

raintree
a Capstone company — publishers for children

Raintree is an imprint of Capstone Global Library Limited, a company incorporated in England and Wales having its registered office at 264 Banbury Road, Oxford, OX2 7DY – Registered company number: 6695582

www.raintree.co.uk
myorders@raintree.co.uk

Edited by Gena Chester
Designed by Veronica Scott
Picture research by Eric Gohl
Production by Steve Walker
Originated by Capstone Global Library LTD
Printed and bound in China

ISBN 978 1 4747 3719 7
20 19 18 17 16
10 9 8 7 6 5 4 3 2 1

British Library Cataloguing in Publication Data
A full catalogue record for this book is available from the British Library.

Acknowledgements
We would like to thank the following for permission to reproduce photographs: Alamy: Action Plus Sports Images, 22, GPI Stock, 27, ZUMA Press Inc, 29; Capstone Studio: Karon Dubke, 6, 7, 9, 12 (right), 16; Getty Images: Steve Hix, 10; iStockphoto: Alberto Pomares, 19, strickke, 14; Newscom: Reuters/Peter Andrews, 4–5, ZUMA Press/Adolphe Pierre-Louis, 13, ZUMA Press/Douglas R. Clifford, 21, 28, ZUMA Press/J. Gwen Berry, 24; Shutterstock: Christian Bertrand, 20, irin-k, 8 (top), 12 (left), 18, 25, 32, IxMaster (football field background), Krivosheev Vitaly, cover, 1, muzsy, 15, Opka, 8 (bottom)

We would like to thank Crissy Makela for her invaluable help in the preparation of this book.

Every effort has been made to contact copyright holders of material reproduced in this book. Any omissions will be rectified in subsequent printings if notice is given to the publisher.

All the Internet addresses (URLs) given in this book were valid at the time of going to press. However, due to the dynamic nature of the Internet, some addresses may have changed, or sites may have changed or ceased to exist since publication. While the author and publisher regret any inconvenience this may cause readers, no responsibility for any such changes can be accepted by either the author or the publisher.

CONTENTS

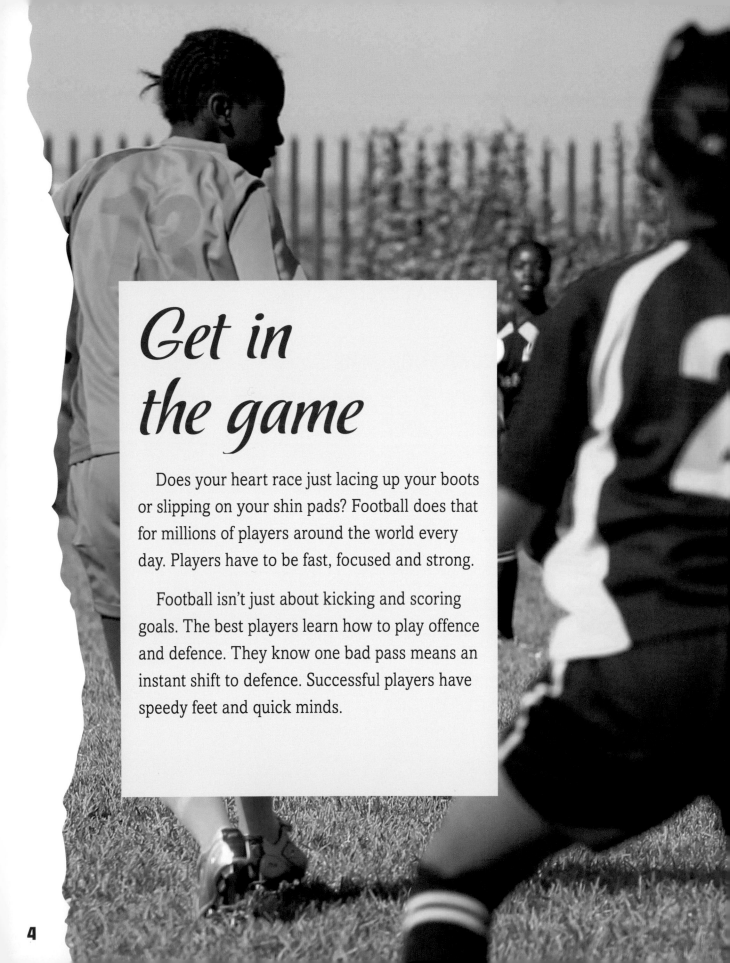

Get in the game

Does your heart race just lacing up your boots or slipping on your shin pads? Football does that for millions of players around the world every day. Players have to be fast, focused and strong.

Football isn't just about kicking and scoring goals. The best players learn how to play offence and defence. They know one bad pass means an instant shift to defence. Successful players have speedy feet and quick minds.

Chapter 1

KICK START
your game

Every football match starts the same way. Two teams of 11 players wait on opposite sides of the halfway line for the referee to blow the whistle. One team kicks the ball to the other team's side. Each team fights to keep the ball. Players use their heads, legs and chests to pass and shoot the ball. Only goalkeepers, or keepers, are allowed to use their arms and hands to touch the ball.

After two halves of play, the team with the most goals wins. If the game is still tied and the league's rules require a winner, teams play two short overtime periods to break the tie. If the game is still tied, each team sends five players to take turns shooting one-on-one at the goal from the penalty mark. If the score remains even, it's time for a heart-pounding shootout where the first team to outscore the opponent in a single round wins.

DRESS FOR *success*

~ Tip ~

If you play on a muddy field, make sure to scrape off mud from your boots after the game. If your shoes are wet inside, stuff them with newspaper to soak up the water.

Football rules require every player to wear football boots, shin pads and knee-high socks along with her team uniform. Goalkeepers also need specially padded gloves to protect their hands and help them grip the ball.

FOOTBALL BOOTS: Football players need to change direction quickly. Rubber spikes help players grip grassy fields and stay on their feet, especially if the grass is wet.

SHIN PADS: These act as leg armor to protect players from injuries. Shin pads have a hard outer layer. Soft padding rests against the skin.

KNEE-HIGH SOCKS: Football socks must cover the shin pads. The socks hold the shin pads in place and help protect other players from the pads' sharp edges.

Football positions

Football players have different roles depending on their positions. Each team has one goalkeeper. The other 10 players are forwards, midfielders and full backs. The number of players in these positions changes by team. Most teams play with four full backs, four midfielders and two forwards.

The fastest players on the team usually are forwards. They score the most goals and spend most of each game in the opponent's half of the field.

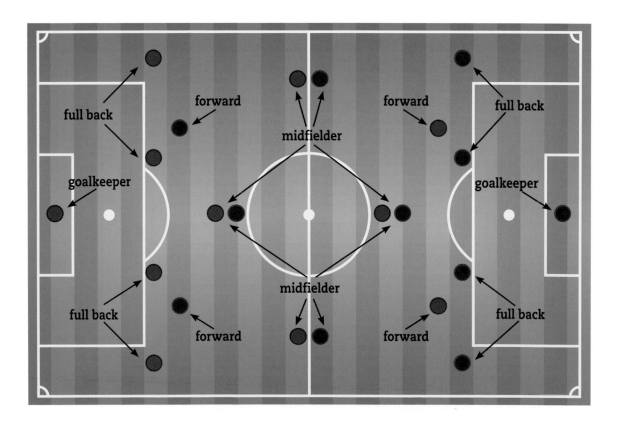

Midfielders start each game behind the forwards. These players, although not always the fastest, run the most. They create plays for the forwards with their sharp passing skills and act as first defenders in **attacks**. Midfielders are also called "mids," "middies" and "halfbacks."

Full backs play defence and protect their goal. They are often the strongest players and out-muscle attackers for the ball. Full backs' strong legs kick the ball far down field to start attacks.

attack offensive strategy designed to score points

elite describes athletes who are among the best

WHERE YOU CAN *play*

If you're new to football, look for a team that meets your needs. Teams form at a range of levels, from local to national. With all of these options, it's easy to find a team that will fit your football skills.

Recreational leagues form teams mostly to play for fun. In these leagues, players learn basic football skills. The leagues assign players to teams without considering their abilities or experience.

School teams usually select players through trials. School teams often travel to other local schools to compete.

Clubs may hold trials to assign players to teams. Many clubs have several different levels of skill and travel to play.

County and national leagues hold trials to select the best players. These teams travel to compete around the country.

Olympic youth football programs seek **elite** players. These teams compete internationally.

Chapter 2

TRAINING
to win

Before teams play games, they work to improve their speed, **stamina** and ball-handling skills. The best players train on their own as well as with their team.

Warm up!

Injury prevention starts with properly warming up muscles before any drill or game. Start with light jogging, skipping or high stepping. Then move to fixed stretches such as toe touches to lengthen muscles. Finish your warm-ups with active stretches such as arm circles, waist-turns and fake kicks.

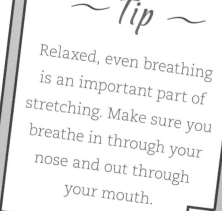

~ *Tip* ~

Relaxed, even breathing is an important part of stretching. Make sure you breathe in through your nose and out through your mouth.

stamina ability to do something hard for a long time

tackle to take away the ball using your feet and legs

The ladder

Players need explosive moves to burst ahead of defenders. Ladder drills improve speed, give players quick feet, and improve footwork for **tackling**. Build your ladder using chalk or tape to make two evenly spaced parallel lines 3 to 5 metres (10 to 15 feet) long. Then draw lines evenly spaced across the two long lines. The distance between the lines should be just bigger than a shoe length. You can think of these lines as the rungs, or steps, of your ladder. Run on the balls of your feet and pump your arms fast. The faster you move your arms, the faster your feet will go. Start facing forwards and run through your ladder taking two small steps between each line. Repeat facing both left and right as you run your ladder.

EATING *to win*

Football players' bodies work hard. They need to refuel with healthy foods. Choosing the right foods, how much and when to eat plays an important part in both training and recovery.

CARBOHYDRATES: Carbohydrates such as whole grains give players' muscles enough energy to keep working for the entire game. Energized players reduce the risk of losing their balance or twisting their ankles due to exhaustion.

PROTEINS: Found in lean meats, nuts and beans, proteins help build and repair muscles. People's bodies can only use so much protein per day. If they eat more than needed, their bodies store extra protein as fat.

FATS: Healthy fats provide energy and help bodies take in vitamins and protect organs. Bodies use more energy to digest high-fat foods like hamburgers. This leaves players sluggish. Instead athletes should eat almonds or baked salmon, which are sources of healthy fats.

Chapter 3

FAST *forwards*

Forwards score the most goals of any position. That's their job. They score goals because they're fast and make **one-touch** passes and shots. If forwards find their first passing options blocked, they move to create other opportunities. Drills for forwards focus on ball-handling skills.

Throwing in the ball

Forwards restart play after the ball goes out of bounds. They use **throw-ins** to get the ball to their teammates. Stand with your hips facing the direction you want the ball to go. Hold the sides of the ball with your fingertips and place your thumbs so that they're just touching behind the ball.

one-touch technique in which a ball is shot or passed from one player to another with one touch, and without stopping

throw-in technique for restarting the game when the ball crosses the sideline and goes out of bounds; a select player throws the ball back in bounds from behind the sideline using both hands

Heading the ball

Forwards **head** the ball when a pass or kick flies in high. When heading the ball, keep your eyes open. Watch the ball all the way to make contact at the hardest spot on the head – the forehead right at the hairline.

Passing to the goal

Forwards always look to pass the ball to an open teammate. Passing moves the ball down the field faster than running with it. Force the defender to chase you by moving to make yourself open for a pass. Moving the ball straight down the field makes the defenders' job easy. Instead, zigzag towards the goal, forcing defenders to change direction.

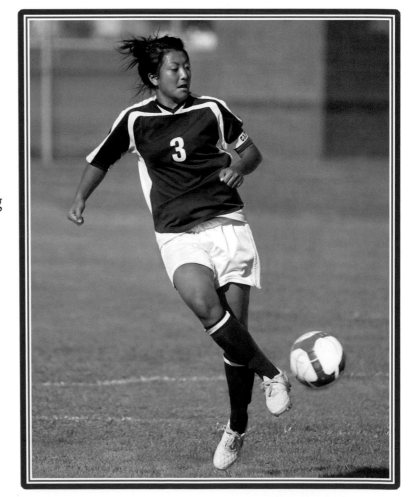

head to hit the ball with your head

Wall ball

No friends to train with? No problem! All you need is a ball and a wall. You can practise passing, kicking and heading using an outside or gym wall. Stand about 1 metre (3 feet) from the wall. Kick the ball with the inside of your foot towards the wall. Practise controlling the rebound off the wall and repeat several times with each foot. Don't forget to practise with the inside and outside of both feet.

~ Tip ~

When you kick, always point your plant foot toes towards your target. Keep your eyes on the ball and watch your kicking foot follow through the ball.

Beating the defence

Forwards aren't the only clever players on the field. If a forward runs the same centre route towards the goal for every attack, defenders quickly learn where to go for the tackle. Forwards need to be masters of **feinting**. They pretend to do the same old run to the goal, but then fake left or right and head to the corner instead. They are also masters at changes in speed as a way to beat a defender.

~ Tip ~

When receiving a pass, pretend the ball is a large raw egg. Relax your body to cushion the ball and keep it from bouncing off. Bend your knees slightly to keep your balance upon impact.

One-touch shooting

Chances of scoring increase if you shoot the first time you touch the ball. Grab a football buddy and head to the field to work on your receiving and shooting skills with this one-touch drill. One player stands in front of the goal. The other passes the ball from the right side. Run to the passed ball. Plant your non-kicking foot in the direction you want to send the ball. Use the inside of your kicking foot for the most control. One-touch shoot, and score! Once you've mastered the right side, switch to your left.

feint to move in a way that confuses or tricks an opponent

SAY *what?*

Winning football teams use certain words to communicate quickly with one another during games. Here are a few words you might hear.

WORD	WHAT YOU'RE TELLING YOUR TEAMMATE
BALL	the ball is coming her way
CENTRE	the ball is going to the middle of the field
CLEAR	you are kicking the ball as far away from your goal as possible
CROSS/SWITCH	you are passing the ball across the field
FOLLOW	a reminder to rush the goal after a shot
FREE	you are open for a pass
KEEP	let the goalkeeper get the ball (only the goalkeeper calls this)
LEFT/RIGHT	where to pass
LINE	pass down the sideline
MAN-ON	defender is coming for a tackle

Chapter 4

MASTER
play-makers

If anyone has eyes in the back of his or her head, it would be a football midfielder. Middies pay attention to the entire field. They know where all of the players on both teams are and where the ball is at all times. Smart middies check over both shoulders to see what's happening around them.

If a team controls the middle of the field, it usually wins. Midfielders take every opportunity to win the ball back, plug holes in the defence and make accurate passes to attackers. They run the entire game and need to be very fit.

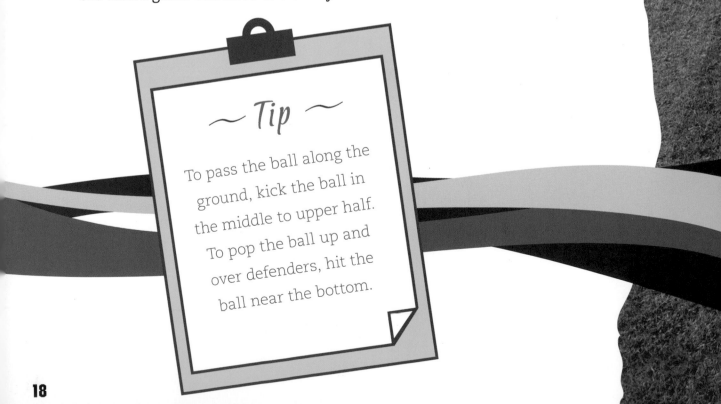

~ Tip ~

To pass the ball along the ground, kick the ball in the middle to upper half. To pop the ball up and over defenders, hit the ball near the bottom.

Plan A to plan B

Midfielders **anticipate** what they are going to do with the ball – should they pass, dribble or shoot? Midfielders have backup plans ready. So if their passing chance gets covered by the defence, they may dribble to an open spot. Smart mids know waiting to decide until they get control of the ball is often too late to make a decision.

Run the Goal

Practise your run on goal with a friendly forward. Fake left and go right. One-touch pass and kick to your partner. Use diagonal passes. Pass with the insides and outsides of both feet. These skills freeze the defenders and make them change directions.

THE MIDFIELD *mix*

Midfielders may have roles they specialize in.

DEFENSIVE: This player helps her team's defence. She reads the opposition and anticipates attacks. She tackles well and is fearless when going in for the steal.

CENTRAL: Teams usually have two central midfielders working together. They intercept passes midfield and run more than the rest of their team. Central midfielders stay calm under constant pressure and make simple passes.

ATTACKING: This player competes on the offensive and sets up offensive plays for the score. She dribbles and receives well. She may score goals for her team.

SIDE OR WINGER: This player sets up attacks on goal by passing the ball from the sidelines to the centre for attackers. She has excellent shielding, receiving, passing and dribbling skills.

~ *Tip* ~

Because midfielders are always under pressure, they use their bodies to **shield** the ball when dribbling. Shielding gives midfielders more time to find an open teammate.

anticipate to think ahead about what may happen

shield to protect the ball from an opponent by positioning yourself between your opponent and the ball

Chapter 5

DEFENDERS
have your back

Keepers depend on defenders to limit the offence as much as possible. Defenders need light feet and great technique to keep up with their opponents. They stay low, **pivot** and change direction quickly. Their arms stay out to their sides for balance. It's important for defenders to be ready to move in all directions, including shuffling backwards. They match quick moves from the offence by staying on their toes.

Defenders excel at reading attackers. Like great scientists, they observe. They can learn which attackers always pass to the right. They see who always fakes right, and then dribbles left. The best defenders use this knowledge against the other team. Defenders work together as a group to prevent goals. They stay close to their **marked** players to shut down passing lanes.

Best foot forwards

Most players shoot and pass more with their stronger foot. Smart defenders force an attacker to go to her weaker foot, which results in bad touches. They take advantage of ball-handling mistakes to win the ball back.

Practise taking away an attacker's stronger side to pass or shoot. Stand just outside the penalty box. Have a right-footed friend dribble the ball in for an attack from midfield. Run towards her in a curved path to your left, which is her right side. As you get closer to her, angle your body sideways to hers. Now she must continue left or be tackled with a poke from your forward foot.

~ Tip ~

Determine which foot an attacker prefers by watching the other team warm up. Don't wait until you're one-on-one during the game.

---

pivot to turn only moving one leg

marked a closely guarded attacker in one-on-one defence

Defensive edge

Defenders must practise patience. When the offence takes a large step, becomes off balance, or loses control of the ball, defenders pounce. They should only make tackles when the ball-handlers make mistakes. Otherwise ball-handlers could run past them.

Defenders can use the sidelines to their advantage. The sidelines take away passing and shooting options. Attackers have less space to dribble the ball and may hand over the ball by kicking it out of bounds. The defender gives her team a chance for a throw-in to start a run on goal.

~ Tip ~

Watch the ball carrier's eyes. She will often look in the direction she wants to pass or shoot.

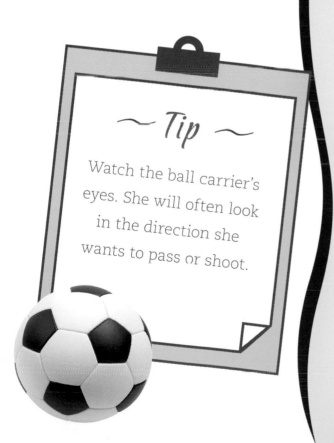

CLEAN *your room*

For this drill, you'll need four or five friends to help. Set up a 14 x 14-metre (15 x 15-yard) box marked with chalk, tape or cones. This is the "room". Pick one or two friends to be on defence and in charge of cleaning their room. Everyone else grabs a ball and dribbles inside of the box. The room cleaners' job is to steal and kick every ball as far out of the box as possible. The dribblers must retrieve their balls and try to get back into the box. The drill is over when every ball is out of the box at the same time.

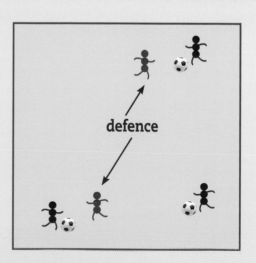

defence

Chapter 6

PROTECT
the goal

Goalkeepers don't just hang out in the net until the other team takes shots on goal. Keepers act as the entire team's eyes. They see the whole field and know what's happening every second. And they don't keep it to themselves either. Keepers shout quick, clear updates to warn teammates of sneaky opponents and open passing lanes.

Goalkeepers face hard shots on goal. They have to throw their bodies in front of speeding balls without hesitation. One mistimed leap or fumbled catch can lead to losing the game. Keepers must let go of their frustration from past goals and instead learn from their mistakes. Although keepers can't stop all shots, the strongest and best believe in themselves to make the next save.

~ Tip ~

Stay on your feet as long as possible. Only dive as a last resort. Make the attacker choose a direction to shoot.

Skills to keep

Sometimes the only thing between you and a shooter is open air. Keep these things in mind to help you block her shot. Stay on the balls of your feet with knees bent to increase leaping heights and reaction speeds for saves. For shots on goal, move towards the ball to leave less shot options. Watch the hips of a shooter for directional clues. If a right-footed shooter's hips are square to goal, she will shoot the ball to the right.

Catching the ball

Once you meet the shot, you have to stop the ball. Spread your hands in a "W" shape with thumbs touching when you catch the ball above your waist. For below-waist shots, turn your "W" upside-down with little fingers touching. Bend your knees and place your hands near the ground with palms forwards and little fingers glued together for ground shots. Anticipate hard shots on goal or wet balls that may slip through your hands by putting your body between the goal and the ball.

When the shot on net is too high for you to catch, make a fist and punch the ball away from the net. Use the flat surface your clenched fingers create to strike the ball up field and towards the sidelines.

~ Tip ~

Sometimes shots are too high for a punch. Use your open palm and fingertips of one hand to tip the ball outside of the goalposts or over the crossbar.

MEET *the ball*

This drill teaches you to meet the ball and then immediately fall back into position for another attack. Stand in the middle of the goal ready to block shots. Have a friend set up a little behind the corner of the penalty box with a ball. A second friend will wait at the edge of the box with another ball.

The first person will kick her ball across the box towards the opposite corner of the net. Meet the shot with a catch, or punch the ball clear of the goal. Immediately return to your position to block a shot from the second person. Once you get the hang of it, continue so the shots are varied every time.

No matter what position you play, football is all about speedy feet and quick thinking. The best players never stop learning and trying to improve. But they also know it's more important to have fun and be a good teammate.

GLOSSARY

anticipate to think ahead about what may happen

attack offensive strategy designed to score points

elite describes athletes who are among the best

feint to move in a way that confuses or tricks an opponent

head to hit the ball with your head

marked closely guarded attacker in one-on-one defence

one-touch technique in which a ball is shot or passed from one player to another with one touch, and without stopping

pivot to turn only moving one leg

shield to protect the ball from an opponent by positioning yourself between your opponent and the ball

stamina ability to do something hard for a long time

tackle to take away the ball using your feet and legs

throw-in technique for restarting the game when the ball crosses the sideline and goes out of bounds; a player throws the ball back in bounds from behind the sideline using both hands

FIND OUT MORE

The Roar of the Lionesses: Women's Football in England,
Carrie Dunn (Pitch Publishing, 2016)

50 Football Skills (Usborne, 2014)

Here Come the Girls, Helen Pielichaty
(Collins Educational, 2012)

WEBSITES

http://www.thefa.com/womens-girls-football
Discover everything you need to know about women's
football in the UK and find a club near you.

http://www.bbc.co.uk/programmes/p04b120r
Watch what is possibly the fastest goal in
woman's football.

INDEX